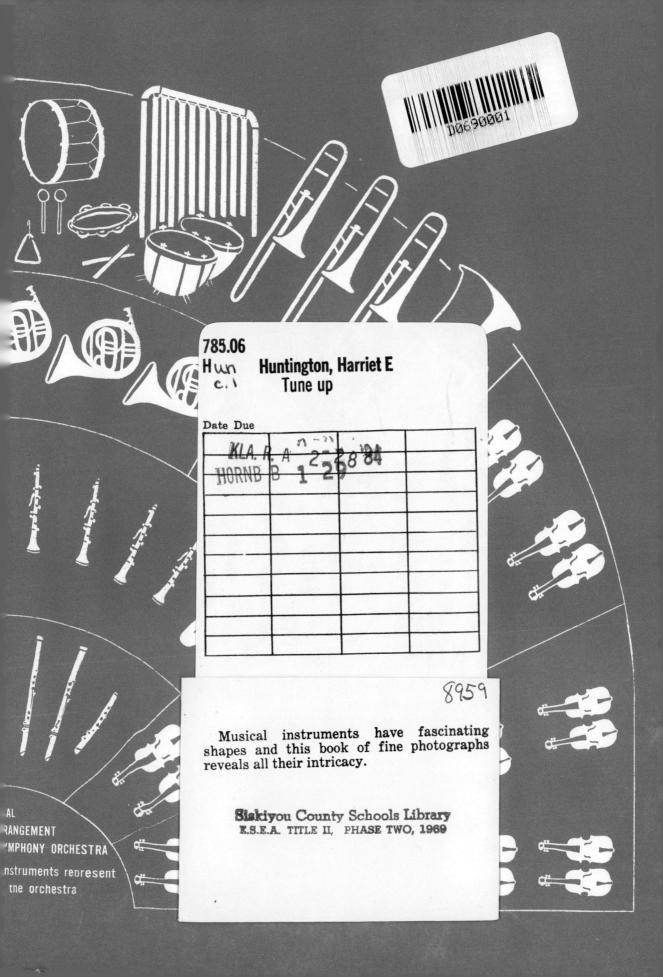

AL
RANGEMENT
MPHONY ORCHESTRA

nstruments represent
tne orchestra

TUNE UP

BOOKS BY HARRIET E. HUNTINGTON

#8859

TUNE UP

THE INSTRUMENTS OF THE ORCHESTRA
AND THEIR PLAYERS

By **HARRIET E. HUNTINGTON**

ILLUSTRATED WITH PHOTOGRAPHS BY THE AUTHOR

FOREWORD BY **ERNEST LA PRADE**

DOUBLEDAY & CO., INC.,   GARDEN CITY, NEW YORK

CONTENTS

FOREWORD

Musical instruments are as varied in form as in quality of tone. Most of them are purely functional in design. Some are simple and some are complex; some are symmetrical and some are not; some are graceful and some are clumsy; but all are objects of interest, particularly to the eyes of youth. Children are fascinated by their peculiar shapes and methods of performance, and many a music lover can trace the birth of his affection to curiosity aroused by his first sight of that bewildering array of instruments which constitutes a symphony orchestra.

In this book Miss Huntington does something more than reproduce the visible characteristics of the orchestral instruments. She shows them, most fittingly, in the hands of attractive young performers — where they are so often found in this era of school orchestras — and she takes advantage of their decorative possibilities to make pictures of intrinsic artistic value and imaginative quality. Through the magic of the lens she succeeds in conveying a suggestion of the esthetic enjoyment which these beguiling contrivances hold for the ear. "Tune Up" should be a source of pleasure and instruction for any child, whether "musical" or not.

ERNEST LA PRADE

PERCUSSION INSTRUMENTS

Haven't you often knocked together two blocks of wood
and liked the noise they made?
That is probably the way man first thought of a drum.
He knocked two large sticks together.
Sometimes he waited a few seconds between knocks.
Knock wait, knock wait, knock wait.
This is a rhythm.
Later, when he wanted to make a louder knock,
he may have hollowed out logs
and beat them with a stick.
Still later he stretched an animal's skin
across the end of the log.
Then he had a drum
and man had one of his first musical instruments.
A drum is called a percussion instrument
because percussion means to strike.
So instruments that are struck like drums or tambourines
belong to the percussion family of instruments.

Even today the American Indian and other primitive peoples
still make drums in the old way.
The primitive drums are called tomtoms,
because the drum sounds tummmm tummmm.
When we use the tomtom in orchestras
we think of primitive people beating out rhythms,
dancing around in circles.
When the head of a drum is struck
it moves slightly but very fast.
This is called vibration.
Sounds are made by vibrations
because vibrations make the air move in waves.
These waves are called sound waves.

Who would think that a drum has a head?
It is the skin stretched across the frame.
The snare drum has skin stretched across both ends.
So the snare drum has two heads.
The snare drum is so named because of the snares
or strings of catgut stretched tightly across the drum head.
The snare drum player beats out his rhythms
on the top drum head with two thin sticks.
Ratta, tat tat, ratta, tat tat.
Drums are used to mark time.
So when the snare drum is played
we think of soldiers marching or hundreds of feet going,
left foot, right foot, left foot, right foot,
parading gayly down the street.

The bass drum is four times larger than the snare drum.
The bass drum is played with one stick.
But there are different sticks for different tones.
The end of one stick is covered with lamb's wool
to give a soft sound.
The end of another stick is covered with felt
to give a medium sound.
The end of still another stick is covered with leather
to give a harsh sound.
The bass drum goes boom, boom, booooom.
Sometimes, when the music grows faster,
the bass drum beats faster;
this makes the music exciting.
And it sounds like cannons shooting one after the other —
boom, boom, boom.

This drum is called a kettle drum
because its bottom is made of copper
and looks like a round kitchen pot.
The head is of calf skin.
This skin is loosened or tightened by six to eight screws.
This stretching gives a different note
when the player beats it.
There are usually two kettle drums in a symphony orchestra.
The larger is tuned to a low note.
The smaller is tuned to a higher note.
The kettle drum is played with two drumsticks.
The heads or balls of these sticks
are covered with lamb's wool or felt.
For very loud sounds
only drumsticks with leather heads are used.
First one stick hits the drum, then the other —
bom, bom, bom, bom, bom, bom, bom.
When this is done fast it is called a "roll."
This is like a roll of thunder,
or someone becoming very angry.
If the "rolls" are loud and fast
they sound exciting.
If the "rolls" are soft and slow
they sound mysterious or scary.

A gong is made of brass.
It is played with a cloth-covered drumstick.
It gives a deep, metallic crash-boom.
Can you guess why a gong is suspended
or held up in the air, dangling from a cord?
If it were not free to vibrate
it would have a dull sound,
not a clear, lasting tone.
You remember vibrations make sound.
Kettle drums can sound like a loud roll of thunder,
but gongs sound like a single clap of thunder
crashing and echoing in the mountains.

Here is a picture of a tambourine.
It is made of a circle of wood like a small hoop
with skin or paper stretched tautly over one side.
Along both sides of this band of wood
are little round pieces of metal that jingle together
when the tambourine is shaken by one hand
or beaten with the other.
Shake, jingle, knock, thud, jingle,
shake, jingle, knock, thud, jingle.
The tambourine is a merry instrument.
Tambourines were first used by gypsies when they danced.
So when a tambourine is played
we picture people having a gay time.

Long ago man thought that if he clapped together
two pieces of metal he could make a very loud noise.
He did, and he had cymbals.
Cymbals are two round plates of brass.
They have leather straps for handles,
so that they can vibrate freely.
In the orchestra, cymbals are struck together
with a sliding motion.
Crashing, crashing, crashing.
Their tone is piercing.
Often the "crashing" marks the end
of a piece of music.
Sometimes it sounds like
a short clap of thunder.

The dancers in northern Africa and Spain
wore tiny cymbals on their fingers.
From the finger cymbals have developed
the wooden castanets which Spanish dancers now use.
A castanet is made of two pieces of wood.
These pieces of wood are hit together to make a clack.
Castanets used in the orchestras are fastened to sticks,
one securely and the other hinged.
When the stick is shaken by the hand
the movable part of the castanet strikes the part fixed to the stick.
A dancer's castanets are tied to the thumb of each hand.
The castanet held in the left hand is the lower in tone.
It is played by moving the wrist back and forth.
The castanet held in the right hand is the higher in tone.
It is played with four fingers, one at a time.
So when castanets are played we think of dancers
whose hands are clapping out rhythms.

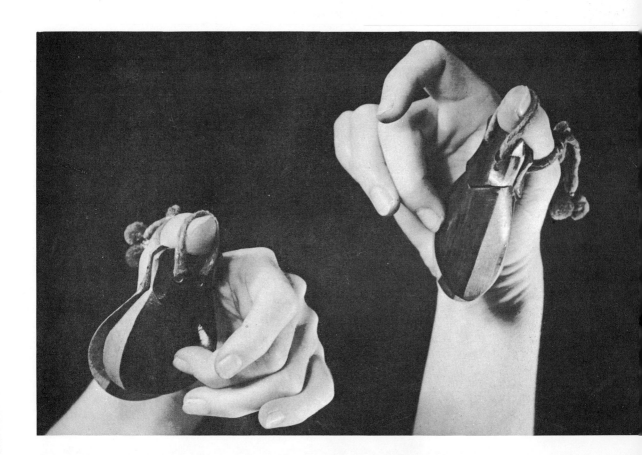

This is a triangle.
It got its name beause of its shape.
It is made of one rod of steel.
This rod is bent twice to form a triangle.
The ends do not touch each other.
The triangle is suspended like a gong
so that it can vibrate.
It is played with another steel rod.
which strikes the three sides.
The triangle sounds like a bell
continuously blown by a breeze.
Tinkling, tinkling, tinkling.
When we hear a triangle played
we are reminded of stars twinkling
or rain falling gently.

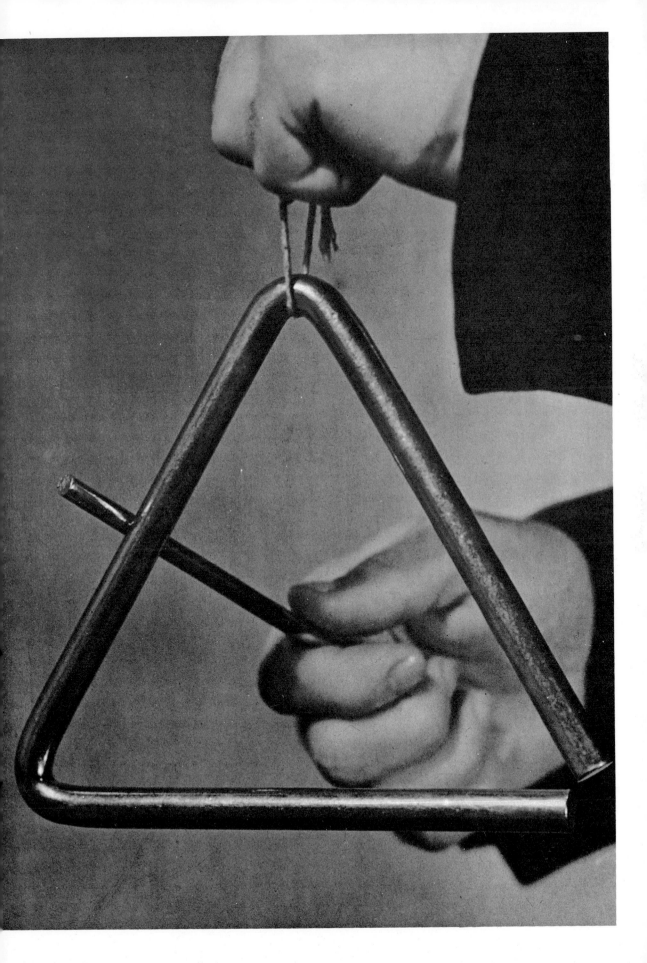

The chimes are pipes made of brass
which are nickel or chromium plated
and are strung up on a bar.
These pipes are different lengths
to give different notes.
They are struck with a rawhide hammer
and sound like bells.
Ting, tong, ting, tong, ting, tong.
When the chimes are played
we think of ringing church bells
or clocks chiming the hours.

The xylophone has pieces of wood
strung in a row across a box.
This box is called a sounding board.
It makes the tones sound louder.
The pieces of wood rest on belts of felt
and are of different lengths to give different notes.
The pieces of wood are struck
with two small wooden hammers.
The xylophone has a bright, brittle tone
which is not lasting like that of a cymbal.
When the xylophone is played
we can imagine dwarfs dancing
because its tones are woody, light, and short.

WOODWIND AND BRASS INSTRUMENTS

It was a long time after man made
his first percussion instrument
until he invented his second musical instrument.
Man found that when he blew through
shells, bones, or horns of animals
he could make a louder noise than he could by yelling.
Later man blew through a hollow grass stalk called a reed.
He found that if he put holes in the reed
he could make higher and lower tones.
He could hold his fingers over the holes,
lifting up the finger over the hole or note he wanted to play.
And so man made tunes.
We have divided the blown instruments into two groups.
Instruments that are blown through and
were once made of wood, like flutes and oboes,
are called woodwinds.
Instruments that are blown through and
are now made of brass, like horns and trumpets,
are called brasses.

WOODWIND GROUP

The flute developed from the ancient reed.
Although the flute is now made of silver
it belongs to the woodwind group of blown instruments.
This is because flutes were originally made of wood,
and even today some primitive peoples
make their flutes of wood or cane.
The flute's straight, hollow tube is two feet long.
The holes in the side which once man's fingers covered
now have little caps.
The flute is one of the most expressive members
of the woodwind family.
It has even been called the coloratura soprano
of the woodwinds because of its high, brilliant tones.
Sometimes its notes seem to dance and skip.
At other times they are full of sweetness, or soft and sad.
Through the centuries the flute has been used
to express emotions as widely varied
as the call to battle,
the shepherd's call to his flocks,
or an Indian love song.

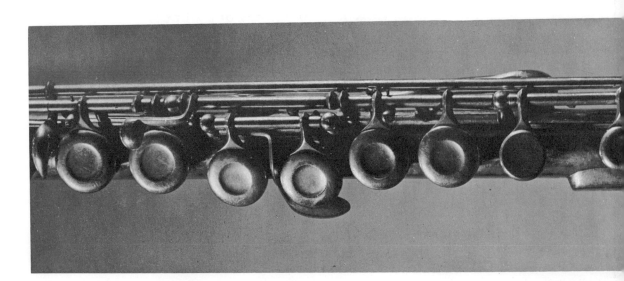

Piccolo means small in Italian.
A piccolo flute is a small flute
but it is usually called piccolo for short.
Its tone is an octave higher than a flute's.
Sometimes it sounds like a bird's call
or like wind whistling around corners and through trees.
The tubes of both the flute and the piccolo
are closed at the upper end.
The mouthpiece is a little way down the tube.
Both these instruments are played
by blowing across the mouthpiece.
Of course some of the air enters the tube,
and it is this air vibrating that makes the tones.

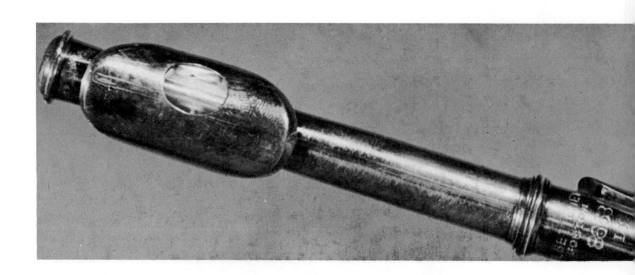

Shepherds made many kinds of flutes.
To the mouthpiece of one kind
they added a thin piece of wood, called a reed.
They opened the upper end of the tube.
From this flute developed the clarinet.
The clarinet's tube has a flared bell at the end.
The clarinet is the singer of the woodwinds.
It can play more tones that are higher
and more tones that are lower
than most of the woodwind instruments.
When we hear a clarinet played
we have a feeling of the outdoors.
Its high tones are clear like the sky.
Its medium tones are noble like the mountains.
Its low tones are deep like the ocean.

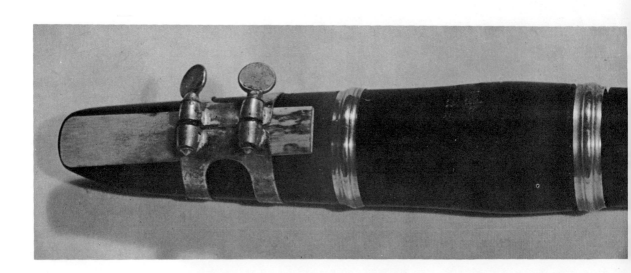

The bass clarinet is like a clarinet only twice as large,
and instead of being straight
its mouthpiece and bell are curved.
Its tone is deeper and mellower than a clarinet's tone.
When it is played the tones remind us of things happening—
such as the moving of clouds in the sky
or perhaps ocean waves pounding and echoing against rocks.

It takes time to learn to blow an oboe
and not make it sound squeaky.
This is because the oboe has two reeds in the mouthpiece.
The oboe reed is something like
a soda straw flattened at one end
and the breath must pass between these reeds.
The oboe is made of hard wood.
Because of the two reeds
it is called a double reed woodwind.
The oboe's tones are sad and sound nasal.
When the oboe is played you may think
of fog creeping and spreading over rolling hills
because it sounds mysterious and weird.

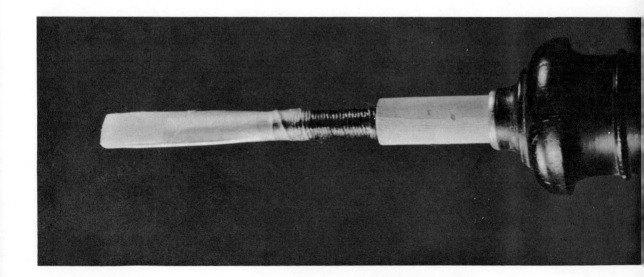

The English horn, or *cor anglais*,
looks and is somewhat like an oboe.
It isn't a horn but a woodwind.
Its mouthpiece's tube is curved
and the bell is rounded.
Its tone is lower, sweeter, and sadder
than an oboe's tone.
These low tones may have
different meanings for different listeners,
just as all music has,
but the English horn often gives
the feeling of snow-capped mountains colored
by the faint glow of a cold northern sunset.

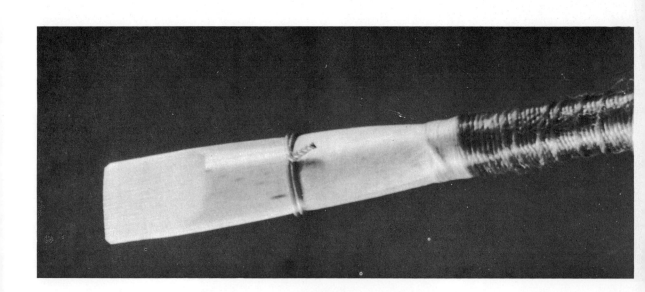

The bassoon has a tube about eight feet long,
but it has been doubled or
folded together like a bundle of sticks
to make the instrument easier to handle.
Of course because it is larger and longer than the oboe
it is deeper in tone.
Like the oboe, it has a double reed.
Really it is a big oboe with a very deep voice.
The bassoon's role in music is sometimes one of comedy,
and its notes indicate funny people
or comic things happening
because it has a funny deep sound as though
someone were singing in the bottom of an empty well.
But this deep tone can also have
a more serious and foreboding quality.

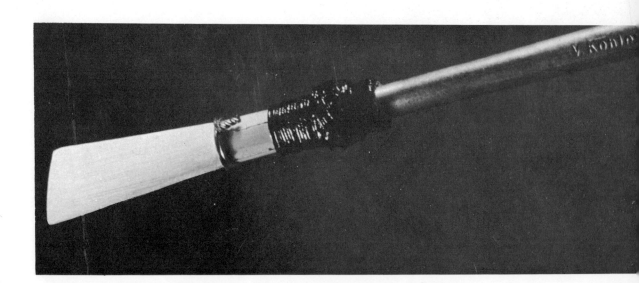

The contra bassoon is a very big bassoon.
Its tube is sixteen feet long,
and even though this tube is folded several times
it is clumsy to hold
Its tone is very, very deep.
When the contra bassoon is played
it echoes and rumbles
like the growling of a huge beast in a cave.

BRASS GROUP

The trumpet belongs to the brass group of blown instruments
because it is made of brass.
Did you know that the bell of a trumpet
is the large outcurving end?
The trumpet has developed from the horn
used by men who lived long ago.
In the olden days trumpets were used
to summon people to hear the king's commands
and today it still gives us the feeling
that it is calling people together.
It has a very loud, brassy tone
but it can be sweet and soft,
depending on the use of the valves and keys.
Sometimes a mute is put in the bell
for a muffled or nasal tone.
The mute is shaped like a pear and is made of metal
on which are glued small pieces of cork or leather
to keep the mute in place.

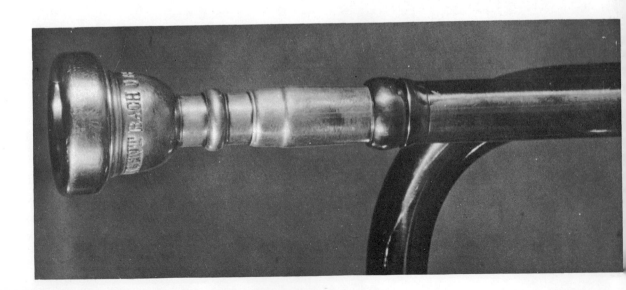

Trombone means big trumpet,
and that is what it really is,
although it has no valves or keys.
The different notes of the trombone are made
by lengthening or shortening the brass tube.
This is done by stretching out or drawing in the arm
so that the tube slides in and out.
Really this tube is two tubes —
an outside tube and an inside tube which fit into each other.
The sound of a trombone is like a great wind singing —
for its loud tones are terribly strong.
But a trombone can be soft too.
For the soft tones the player uses a mute
like the pear-shaped trumpet mute only larger.

This brass instrument is called a French horn
because it was first developed by the French kings
for elaborate hunting calls.
This paved the way for its use in the orchestra.
The valves open or close parts of the tube
to make it long or short.
Because hunters liked to call to one another
the tube was originally curled
so that it could be worn around the neck
and the hunters could carry it
without using their hands.
Like the trumpet, the horn can be muted.
Its tones are deeper than the trumpet's.
When we hear the French horn
we almost feel as though the soft, sweet, clear notes
were echoing from hill to hill and down the valleys
as the hunters signal to each other
while riding after the hounds.

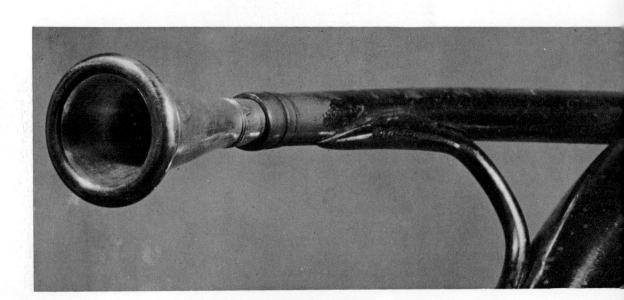

The tuba's tube is so long that
it has to be curled around and around several times.
Certainly the tuba would look funny
if it were stuck straight out,
to say nothing of carrying an instrument
that was twice as long as a bed.
If you look closely at the picture
you can see that the tuba becomes larger
from the mouthpiece to the bell.
The tuba's tone is very low and quite fearful.
Sometimes when it is played
we think of a dragon moving clumsily about,
as though he had just awakened.

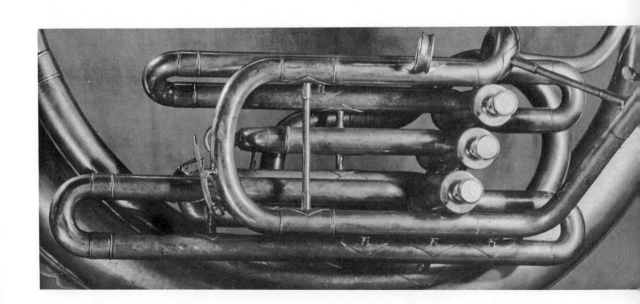

The saxophone is a cross between
a brass and a woodwind instrument.
It is made of brass and has a reed.
Sometimes it is called a woodwind,
but usually it is called a brass instrument.
The saxophone was invented by Antoine Sax
and was named after him.
It has a tone that is loud and brassy but sad.
Sometimes it sounds like people wailing out their grief.
But it can also be comic.
Sometimes its tones sound like a frog croaking.
A saxophone is used mostly in dance bands.
There it sings the blues — music to which we dance.

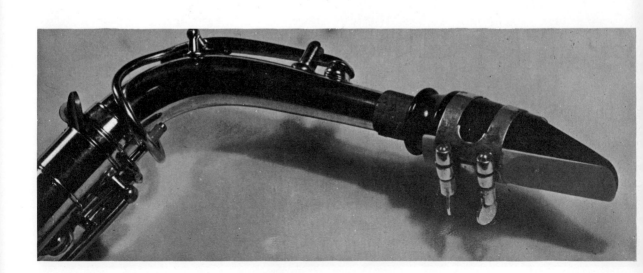

STRING INSTRUMENTS

Man heard a tone after he shot his bow and arrow.
This was because the string vibrated after being pulled
and the vibration made a tone.
Perhaps this was what made man think that
he could put more strings on a bow and play a tune.
At first he used four strings.
This was called a lyre or small harp.
He added a gourd to the bow.
This was like a sounding box.
Later he tried a way of plucking the string with his arrow.
He drew his arrow across the string.
He had a violin,
and man had his fourth musical instrument family—the strings.

The earliest violin had one string.
Now the violin has four strings.
The violin is played by
drawing back and forth across the strings
a thin, narrow stick with horsehair
stretched along its length.
This is called a bow and
is an outgrowth of the arrow
with which man originally plucked the strings.
Different notes are made
by moving the fingers up or down the strings.
These are tuned by four pegs
at the top of the violin.
The sounding box is curved
so that the bow will not hit the sides.
If the bow goes across slowly and evenly
the violin gives a long, even tone.
Sometimes the bow seems to fly about
or saw rapidly back and forth.
Sometimes it dances, or jigs as it strikes the strings
and then the music of the violin dances too.

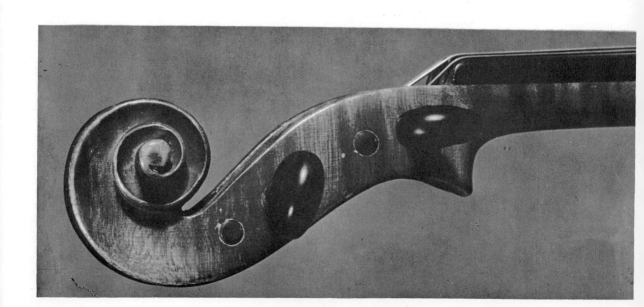

Did you know that a violin had a bridge?
It is a small piece of wood
which holds the strings up and away
from the sounding board,
so that the strings can vibrate freely.
Violins may be muted.
The mute looks like a comb with three teeth.
It is placed over the strings on the bridge.
This makes the tone sad.
Violins are the voice of the orchestra.
In a symphony orchestra
the violins are divided into two sections.
The first group plays the melody.
The second group plays a harmonizing melody.
The violin can make us happy or sad,
for the violin can describe
almost any sound its player wishes.
The viola is a violin only just a little bigger,
and a little deeper in tone,
but it can play four tones lower.

The violoncello is really a still larger violin.
It is so big that
the sounding box is held between the player's legs.
It has a deep, rich, strong tone.
Like the violin's, the cello's sweet tones
seem to speak to us, particularly of strength and beauty.

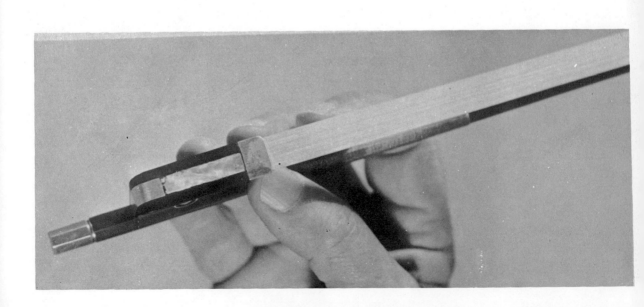

The double bass is also called a bass viol.
It is so large that to play it
a man has to stand up or sit on a high stool.
The larger an instrument
the lower and deeper the tones.
The bass viol can sound comic when it is played fast,
but usually its tone is solemn or full of anger.

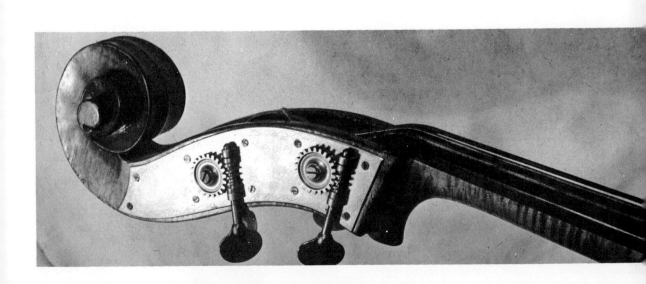

The harp is a beautiful-looking instrument,
often decorated with gold.
The harp has forty-six strings.
Each string is tuned by a key,
which turns the string's peg.
The tones from the strings can be made
sharper or flatter by the use of pedals.
These are moved by the player's feet.
Like the ancient harp, the strings are plucked
so that they vibrate.
The player uses both hands.
Sometimes the player takes one finger
and draws it up, around and down.
This is called "glissando"
and sounds like rain falling.
When a harp is played it has a liquid, airy tone
that reminds us of brooks, waterfalls,
and clouds floating in the air.

The piano is a combination of
a stringed instrument and a percussion instrument.
Inside its large outer case
it has strings like those of a harp,
but they are laid flat over the piano's sounding board.
It is these strings which make the piano
belong to the string family of instruments.
The piano has a row of flat keys, the keyboard.
Some of the keys are colored black and some white
to make it easier to tell the notes apart.
Each key when struck by a finger
brings forth a different note,
for each key in turn makes a little felt hammer
hit one of the strings.
Because its hammers hit the strings
the piano is also related to the percussion family.
The piano has three pedals,
which make the tones louder, softer, or more lasting.
A piano can play eighty-eight notes
more than any other instrument.
On it can be played music that is happy, sad,
gay, angry, loving, or worshipful.

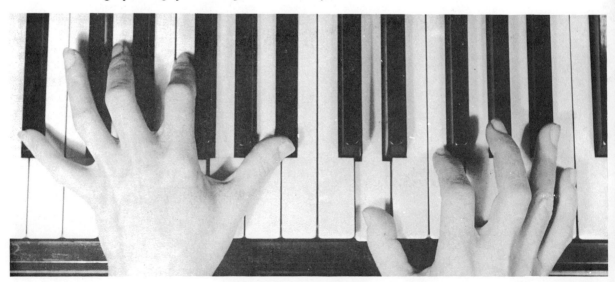

Man tied together side by side several
flutes of different lengths.
This was called the pipes of Pan.
An organ is a tremendous pipes of Pan.
Small organs have hundreds of pipes.
Big organs have thousands of pipes.
The pipes usually are made of metal
graduated from one foot to fifteen feet in height.
The largest pipes, made of wood, are square.
Sometimes they are thirty feet high.
An organ is played by means of
several keyboards, called manuals.
Each manual is back and above the other.
Electric wires go from the keys to the pipes
to open or close the valves of each pipe.

The air is blown into the pipes
by an electric bellows.
There is also a pedal keyboard.
This is worked by the player with his feet.
An organ has many "stops" or levers
which make separate instrument sounds—
like violins, oboes, flutes, drums, and even a human voice.
An organ is a complicated machine
but one that brings forth satisfying music.
The player is really conducting an orchestra.
Although the organ has keys
which are struck like those of a piano,
it belongs in the wind-instrument family
because its sounds are made by the wind in its pipes.

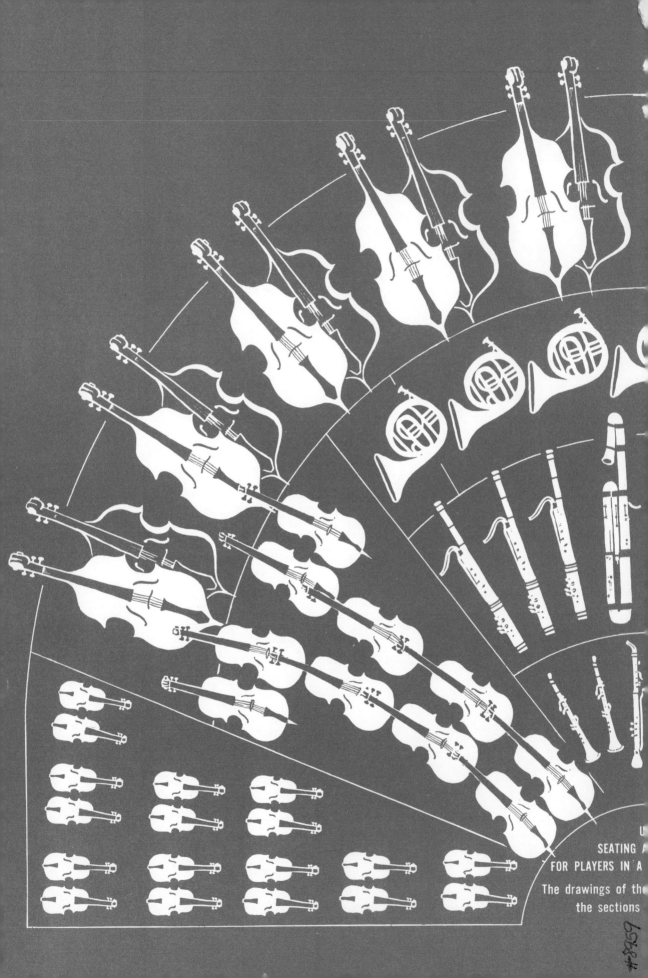

SEATING A
FOR PLAYERS IN A

The drawings of the
the sections